HOW TO USE SELF-CONTROL

by

Karen Esveldt-Dawson, M.A., and Alan E. Kazdin, Ph.D.
Western Psychiatric Institute & Clinic
University of Pittsburgh School of Medicine

ISBN 0-89079-067-1

© Copyright, 1982, by H & H Enterprises, Inc.
946 Tennessee Street
Lawrence, Kansas 66044

Contents

	Page
Foreword	v
Introduction	vi
Self Control	1
With Adults	1
With Adolescents	2
With Children	3
Self-Control Procedures	4
PROCEDURE I—Self-Observation	4
PROCEDURE II—Self-Reinforcement	6
PROCEDURE III—Self-Punishment	9
PROCEDURE IV—Alternate Response Training	12
PROCEDURE V—Stimulus Control	14
PROCEDURE VI—Self-Instruction Training	16
Guidelines For Using Self-Control	20
Monitoring Behavior	21
Handling Problems That Arise	22
Planning Your Own Self-Control Program	23
References	26

Foreword

This publication is one in a series of manuals designed to help persons in various settings learn to use behavioral procedures. It differs somewhat from the other manuals in the series. Most of the manuals present a single concept or procedure intended to help bring about behavioral changes in specific applications with other persons. This manual by Esveldt-Dawson and Kazdin focuses on a single concept (self control) but it presents six different procedures for achieving self control rather than concentrating on a single procedure. Secondly, most manuals in this series are designed to be used by parents, teachers, employers or others to change the behavior of another person. In contrast, this manual concerns the behavior of the reader and thus the reader or user is the primary subject of the behavior change.

This manual fits into the series well because the eventual goal of all the manuals in the series is to help someone engage in appropriate behavior independent of direct supervision. This goal is implicit in all the manuals. Esveldt-Dawson and Kazdin present their self-control procedures in such a simple and direct manner that self control becomes no more complex than most other behavior management concepts.

Like the other manuals, this one is intended to be used under the direction of a qualified professional who can supply feedback, explanation and support in carrying out the procedures. We are delighted to add this manual to this series, and we know it will provide a new and useful tool to persons who are seeking to manage their own behaviors as well as the behaviors of persons with whom they live and work.

R. Vance Hall, Ph.D.
Marilyn C. Hall, Ed.D.

Introduction

The self-control techniques in this book can be used to alter behavior or to maintain behavior after another type of behavior modification program has been withdrawn. Self-control techniques can be used to develop behavior in the classroom, home, institution, and community settings. The different techniques all rely on the clients to carry out specific procedures to alter their own behavior. After an initial period in which the clients learn the techniques, they can apply them where other persons such as parents, teachers or staff may not be available to carry out the procedures.

The different self-control techniques can be used alone or in combination. Also, self-control techniques can be used by themselves or with other behavioral techniques such as systematic attention and approval, planned ignoring, feedback, time out, and procedures described in other manuals in this series. This manual covers different self-control techniques and illustrates their application with different clients, behaviors, and settings. Exercises are provided to help the reader apply the different procedures.

Self-Control

Self-control refers to the process whereby an individual deliberately alters or changes his or her behavior to achieve a specific goal. The individual decides what it is that he or she wants changed and what procedures to use to achieve these changes. A further requirement to qualify as self-control is that the person self-administers these procedures. To illustrate different uses of self-control, some examples of self-control programs are described below.

With Adults

Mary's gas bills for her car grew to $50.00 or $60.00 a month, which was more than she could afford. She already had a small car so she knew she had to do something else. To reduce her gas bills she had to drive less. She could not easily change her drive to and from work every day. She did, however, make lots of little trips almost every day. She decided to keep a record of every time she drove her car to see if she could decrease the number of times she used her car. To help herself, she made up a chart that she kept in the car. On the chart she recorded the date, destination, approximate number of miles, and reason for each trip. During the first week, she recorded 18 trips. By the third week, she was able to use the car only 11 times. The self-observation and recording had helped her eliminate unnecessary trips and combine trips. Her first gas bill following her program was $20.00 less than the previous month. Mary was very pleased with herself.

What was Mary trying to do? _____

_____

_____

Was she successful?_____

Why is this an example of self-control? _____

_____

_____

_____

With Adolescents

"Bill!! You are late again!! Every day it's the same thing — two or three hours late for dinner!" Because of constant arguments and other problems resulting from his tardiness, Bill decided he must do something about getting home on time.

The problem was that on the way home from school each day he walked past the park where his friends played basketball and he couldn't resist getting into the game. As he thought about the problem, he decided that if he would walk home a different way, he wouldn't be tempted to play ball. He then could get home in time for dinner, and his mother wouldn't be mad.

What was Bill trying to do? _____
_____
_____

Was he likely to be successful? _____

How did he plan to use self-control? _____
_____
_____

With Children

During the monthly class discussion in Mrs. Black's sixth-grade class, the students brought up homework and the problems each was having getting homework done each night. They decided to do something about it by having each one keep track of his or her own behavior. They decided that each student would place a check next to the date on his or her own chart each time homework was turned in. At the end of the week, they were to grade themselves according to the following schedule: A = 5 checks, B = 4 checks, C = 3 checks, D = 2 checks, E = 1 check. The children made up their own charts and kept them at their desks. A month later, during the class discussion, homework was no longer one of the problems the class needed to discuss.

Describe what the children did to solve their problem. _____
_____
_____

Was it successful? _____

How did the children use self-control? _____

_____

_____

The above illustrations describe self-control procedures used to either increase desirable behaviors or decrease undesirable behaviors. Describe what self-control means to you.

_____

_____

_____

_____

All of us have at some time applied self-control procedures to our own lives. Sometimes self-control procedures were successful; sometimes they were not. Describe below a situation where you used self-control and it was successful. _____

_____

_____

_____

_____

Why do you feel it was successful? _____

_____

_____

Now, describe another situation where you tried to control your own behavior but the attempt was unsuccessful. _____

_____

_____

_____

_____

_____

_____

_____

Self-Control Procedures

The self-control procedures in this manual follow the basic principles of behavior modification described in previous manuals in this series. These behavior modification procedures usually involve one person being able to change the behavior of another by controlling what precedes or follows the behavior. These same procedures can be applied by individuals to alter and control their own behaviors. Six different self-control procedures are discussed and illustrated with examples. The different procedures are described separately, but they are often combined to insure success. Examples illustrate the combination of different self-control procedures.

PROCEDURE I—Self-Observation

Individuals are usually unaware of the extent to which they perform various behaviors. Habitual behaviors become automatic. When persons are given the opportunity to observe their own behavior carefully, behavior often changes. **Self-observation consists of systematically observing one's own behavior.** The observations do not consist of merely trying to notice what one is doing. Rather, the observations consist of keeping track and scoring how many times a particular behavior is performed. When a person keeps close track of behavior, behavior often improves.

For example, a teacher may be concerned that a child constantly shouts out a question or an answer in class instead of raising his hand. The child may know he is shouting out but not be aware of the extent to which this occurs and how disruptive it is. The teacher may devise a sheet for the child so he can record each time he blurts out a comment. The child could keep a tally to see how often the behavior occurs. Merely observing the frequency of blurting out comments may decrease their frequency.

The exact reasons why self-observation changes behavior are not fully understood. One view is that the observations provide feedback which causes individuals to use other self-control techniques such as self-reinforcement and self-punishment to control their behavior. These other techniques are discussed separately below. However, the important point is that self-observation often alters behavior by itself without other procedures.

Self-observation is critical to most self-control techniques. Self-observation provides basic information about how often the behavior occurs. In self-control techniques, information about the frequency of behavior is crucial for deciding when the individual should provide consequences for behavior. Self-observation can also be used with other techniques such as systematic attention, or praise by others such as a parent or teacher. These other persons can provide reinforcing consequences such as praise for changes in the frequency of the behaviors that the client is observing.

The crucial elements to remember when using self-observation are:
- Identify the behavior in very clear terms so the client can observe its frequency.
- Provide an easy means for the client to record the behavior (such as a checklist or card where a simple tally can be kept).
- Make sure the assessment method or data sheet allows the client to see if the behavior has improved, become worse, or has not changed over time.

With some clients, the responses may even be graphed to allow them to see progress on a daily basis. A graph or similar record of the response is important because other persons may examine the progress and provide reinforcement.

The following example demonstrates the correct use of self-observation as a self-control technique.

Mrs. Blunt slumped down into her chair. She was exhausted and upset. She had spent the entire day yelling at and disciplining her children. She was determined to make things more pleasant for her children and for herself. She decided to get a better idea of how many times each day she paid attention to her children when they were being good. She taped a piece of paper to the refrigerator and marked off the days of the week. Then, throughout each day, she made a mark on the paper whenever the children were good and she interacted with them in a positive way. As the days passed, Mrs. Blunt and her children spent more and more time together in positive situations.

Self-recording the number of times she paid attention to her children for their good behavior helped Mrs. Blunt change her own behavior and the behavior of her children.

Describe what self-observation is._____

_____

_____

You are doing great if you said that self-observation means keeping a record of one's performance of a particular behavior. This record can involve information on when, where, how often, and under what conditions a particular behavior is performed. The choice as to what aspects of a particular behavior to record depends on what you want to monitor and change.

To give you a chance to show how well you understand self-observation, as a self-control technique, a problem situation is presented below. Please read it and describe a self-control plan using self-observation.

The phone rang. It was Skip's friends wanting him to go out with them again. Skip paused for a moment and then said, "Sure, I'll be right over." As Skip hung up the phone, he got a heavy feeling in his stomach. He had his college entrance exams in two months and he knew it would be necessary for him to study for them. When he had worked out what he needed to review, he figured he needed approximately 80 hours of study time to review all of the material. He paused a moment longer and then headed out to be with his friends. "Oh, well," he said to himself, "you can't study all the time."

If you were Skip, describe how you would use self-observation as a self-control technique in this situation. _____
_____
_____
_____
_____

PROCEDURE II—Self-Reinforcement

Many behavior change programs depend upon external agents such as staff, parents, teachers, or peers to provide reinforcing consequences. Most of the procedures described in other manuals in this series are based on procedures carried out by other persons on behalf of the client. However, clients can provide consequences to themselves to increase or decrease the frequency of behaviors. Clients can be trained to administer consequences to themselves for specific behaviors instead of receiving consequences from an external agent.

The major requirement of self-reinforcement is that clients are able to provide rewards to themselves when a particular behavior is performed. Self-reinforcement may be carried out in different ways depending upon what aspects of the reinforcement procedure the client performs. In each variation, the client plays a role in some aspect of delivering the reinforcing consequences. At one extreme, the client may determine what behaviors to reinforce, when to reinforce the behaviors, and the amount of reinforcement that is delivered. At the other extreme, the client may be responsible only for delivering rewards to himself or herself. Other persons decide the behaviors that are to be rewarded and the amount of the reinforcer earned.

The self-reinforcement procedure that is selected may be determined by the client's age, abilities, and target problems. For example, self-reinforcement for young children in a classroom setting often relies on teachers, in varying degrees, to help decide the target behaviors to be reinforced and the amount of reinforcement. If children are left on their own to decide the target behaviors and amount of reward, they might become very lenient and reward themselves without performing the desired behaviors. In all self-reinforcement procedures, clients are given some responsibility for administering the reinforcers for their own behaviors. The extent to which other external agents are involved in assisting the clients in delivering rewards may vary.

As part of self-reinforcement, the client usually engages in self-observation. Self-observation is essential so the client can determine whether the desired behavior has been performed. For example, self-reinforcement and self-observation might be used in the home to reduce inappropriate table manners of children. The children may be instructed to mark each time they speak with their mouths full or get up and reach across the table for food rather than asking for food to be passed to them. Once the observation procedure is devised, the children can be told to give themselves stars or checkmarks for each meal in which they show fewer than a particular number of inappropriate target behaviors. Self-observation permits the children to record the behaviors. Stars are self-administered when the children have not exceeded a particular number of inappropriate behaviors. The stars are exchanged for privileges such as watching a special television show or staying up an extra few minutes later at bed time. The procedure illustrates self-reinforcement because the children give themselves stars for their own performance during or after meals. Depending on the age and abilities of the children, the parents may provide initial assistance in recording the behavior correctly and in providing the stars for appropriate performance. Eventually, the children take over the program with little or no supervision.

The crucial elements to remember about using self-reinforcement are:

- Require the clients to self-observe to obtain information about the frequency of the behavior to be changed.
- Select reinforcers that the clients can easily administer to themselves.
- Specify the behavior or have the clients specify the behavior

that will be reinforced and the amount of the reinforcer that will be provided.

An example of self-reinforcement to change behavior follows:

Katie was going to be starting high school in the fall and she was worried. She had always been overweight but recently she had put on even more weight. She figured that most of the other kids her age didn't want to pal around with an overweight person and that kids who were heavy had a more difficult time with peer relationships and often were excluded from social situations. Besides, who would ask her for a date?

She discussed the problem with her mom, and they decided to try something to help her lose weight. She had tried several crash diets but none of them had worked. This time she was going to eat regular food but less of it. In addition, she realized that she needed an added incentive to help her stay on her diet. She worked out a program for herself where every week she would weigh herself on Friday night. If she had lost 2 pounds that week, she would ask her girlfriend over to do something special on the weekend. Her mom agreed to help by taking them special places, if they wished. Since this was something really special that Katie enjoyed doing, she felt it would be a strong incentive to eat less. After one month Katie had lost six pounds. She had missed only one weekend with her girlfriend and, best of all, she was beginning to look thinner.

By now you should have a good understanding of self-reinforcement. Describe what it means. _____
_____
_____
_____
_____

You should have said that individuals decide what will be their reinforcement, when they will get the reinforcement and what they must do to get the reinforcement. Great job if your answer included those points!

The situation described below needs a self-reinforcement program.

The Hillsdale basketball team was in trouble. The morale of the members was very low. The members did not seem committed to practicing. They would get excited about the games but not for the daily practices. The players lacked the necessary motivation to really benefit from the workouts. Something had to be done before they played many more games.

How could the players use a self-reinforcement program to alter their behavior? _____

_____
_____
_____
_____

PROCEDURE III—Self-Punishment

Self-reinforcement procedures usually are applied to increase a particular target behavior. Yet, sometimes the major interest of the program is to reduce the frequency of a particular behavior. Punishment is used to that end. Self-reinforcement techniques are quite useful, even if the goal is to eliminate behavior. Reinforcement can focus on increasing behavior that is incompatible with the undesired response. For example, if children are not complying with the requests of their parents, a punishment procedure need not be used. Rather than punishing noncompliance, the program may focus on reinforcing compliance to parental requests. Yet, punishment often is a useful adjunct to programs that are managed by parents, teachers, and other behavior-change agents. Self-punishment also can help a self-control program.

Self-punishment consists of having the clients provide aversive consequences to themselves after a particular behavior is performed. As with self-reinforcement, self-punishment requires that the client observe the performance of the target behavior so that the consequences can be applied contingently. The observations provide the information required to decide when aversive consequences should be applied.

Self-punishment has been used infrequently by itself as a behavior change technique for several reasons. As a general rule, it is not desirable to use programs based primarily on punishment. Punishment programs may be associated with undesirable side effects such as crying and aggression. Also punishment programs do not teach the appropriate behaviors that are to be performed. Finally, clients generally do not find punishment programs as acceptable as programs based upon positive reinforcement.

The above disadvantages are associated with punishment procedures in general, if they are not supplemented with reinforcement procedures as well. With self-punishment, there is an added problem. Because clients are responsible for administering the consequences, it is unlikely that they will carry out the program. Clients may be unlikely to continue a self-punishment program for very long because of the undesirable consequences that, by definition, are part of the procedures.

Self-punishment is usually included as part of a program involving self-reinforcement. The effectiveness of positive reinforcement for desirable behavior is often increased by supplementing the program with punishment for undesirable behavior. For example, in a junior high school classroom, adolescents may participate in a program where they administer points to themselves for turning in their homework at the beginning of class or completing arithmetic problems. These behaviors may be associated with self-administration of reinforcement. Other behaviors such as coming to class late, fighting with others, or disrupting the class could be included in the program as part of self-punishment. Performance of these behaviors may require the students to take away points from their earnings because they are not likely to provide punishing consequences as eagerly as they provide reinforcing consequences.

The crucial elements to remember about using self-punishment are:
- Require the clients to self-observe to obtain information about the behaviors that are to be changed.
- Select aversive consequences that the clients can and will administer to themselves when the inappropriate behavior is performed.
- Specify the behavior that will be punished and the specific consequences that will be provided.
- Combine self-punishment with self-reinforcement procedures to ensure that appropriate behaviors are being developed.

Illustrated below is a self-punishment procedure used to alter behavior.

> *Bill had just started a new job. He wanted to do well and he really needed the money to start paying off his school debts. His problem was getting up in the morning and off to work on time. He had been working only two months, and he had been late six times. Something had to change. He decided to set up a punishment program for being late. For each time he was late, he*

decided to send $2.00 to support the campaign of a local official who was running for office. He chose an official whose views did not match his own so that giving up the money would be aversive. Also, he could not afford to send money very often because this would take away from his money for movies and other things he enjoyed. In addition to the punishment program, he provided self-reinforcement. For every week he was on time all of the days, he decided to buy himself a new book because he enjoyed reading very much.

Describe self-punishment as a self-control technique. _____

_____
_____
_____
_____

Self-punishment means that the person, depending upon his or her ability, decides when, where and how aversive consequences are to be applied to reduce undesirable behavior. Pat yourself on the back if your answer was similar to the one above.

The vignette presented below illustrates a situation where self-punishment could be applied:

Mr. Brink had just returned from his physician. He had a persistent cough and had wanted it checked. The doctor informed him that he must stop smoking. But how? He had tried everything including not thinking about cigarettes, counting them and chewing gum instead of having a cigarette — but nothing had worked.

Describe how Mr. Brink might use self-punishment to control smoking. (Be sure to include self-reinforcement as well.) _____

_____
_____
_____
_____
_____
_____
_____

PROCEDURE IV—Alternate Response Training

Another self-control technique is to train the client to engage in behaviors that interfere with or replace another response that he or she is trying to control. The purpose is to replace one response with another or to train an alternate response. People use alternate responses in everyday life to control all sorts of behavior. For example, people often clasp their mouths to stifle a laugh that is inappropriate in a particular situation, cover their eyes to avoid seeing something that is upsetting, or chew gum to avoid smoking cigarettes. In these examples, the individuals engage in one response to control another response.

As a self-control technique, alternate response training involves specifically training another response to replace an undesired behavior. A response is developed that the person can use in a variety of situations to disrupt or replace an undesired response. A common focus of alternate response training is to control anxiety. Adults and children may feel anxious in a variety of situations. With alternate response training, the client is trained to engage in a response that interferes with anxiety. Typically, clients are trained to relax their muscles. Relaxation can be trained in a variety of ways. Some persons alternatively tense and relax their muscles while a trainer encourages them to become deeply relaxed. Clients may make suggestions to themselves to become relaxed. Meditation or imagery of pleasant thoughts are sometimes used to promote relaxation.

Once an alternate response is trained, the client can apply that response to a variety of situations. For example, a person with high blood pressure might learn how to relax and apply the procedure a few times per day while at the office, in his or her car while in traffic, and before going to sleep at night. He or she could also apply the relaxation procedure under special situations that arise when he or she is feeling tense. The procedure is a self-control technique because the person can apply the alternate response as needed in everyday situations.

The crucial elements to remember about using alternate response training are:

- Teach the client a behavior that will interfere with the behavior that is to be altered.

- Check to see that the behavior is well developed and that the client can apply it on his or her own.

An example of alternate response training is described below.

*"Kurt is a **baby**! Kurt is a **baby**!"*
Kurt turned around and started home. He knew how funny he looked when he sucked his thumb. Sucking his thumb had been a problem for the past couple of years, and it was becoming more of a problem as he got older. He would be 9 years old in the fall, and he really wanted to stop. He talked with his mom about what to do. She suggested that everytime he started to suck his thumb, he should try doing something else. They decided that he should carry a supply of candy and gum with him and that whenever he started to put his thumb in his mouth, he would instead take out a piece of gum and chew it or eat a piece of candy. In the beginning, when Kurt was home, his mom helped remind Kurt and praised his attempts. They both knew eating lots of candy was not very good, but if it could help stop the thumbsucking it would be worth it.

It was very hard for Kurt to make himself chew the gum or eat the candy instead of sucking his thumb — but at the end of three weeks, he had significantly reduced the number of times he was thumbsucking.

Explain alternate response training. _____
_____
_____

You did a fine job if your answer said that alternate response training means training a person to perform a different or new behavior that interferes with and replaces the behavior that is to be changed.

To practice applying your new knowledge, a problem situation that could use an alternate response training procedure is described below.

Joan had just accepted a job as a sales representative for the local telephone company. She would be required to do a great deal of flying and that was the problem. Joan hated flying. As soon as she entered the plane, she broke out in a sweat and became so nervous she couldn't eat. Afterward she became sick to her stomach. All she could think about was the terrible things that could happen to the plane. She knew she had to do something to get her mind off crashing.

Describe how Joan could use alternate response training. _____

_____
_____
_____

PROCEDURE V—Stimulus Control

Behaviors are often influenced by various situations, persons, and other events or stimuli in the environment. For example, one behaves differently at home than at school. Also, persons show different table manners at home, at a guest's house, at a formal dinner, or at a fast-food restaurant. The presence of different persons may also lead us to behave differently. For example, children usually speak very differently in the presence of their peers compared to how they speak in the presence of their parents and teachers.

Situational clues influence behavior because of different learning experiences that take place in the presence of these cues. Specifically, a particular behavior is reinforced in some situations but not in others or by some persons and not by others. Eventually, a person learns to perform particular behaviors under very specific circumstances. In a given situation, responses which have been reinforced in the past in that situation are much more likely to be performed. Essentially, the person's behavior is said to be under stimulus control. The stimulus conditions (situation, other persons, setting) determine the responses likely to be performed.

Persons who are aware of how certain stimuli influence behavior can structure their environment to maximize the likelihood that the desired behavior will occur. **The main task of using stimulus control as a self-control technique is to evaluate what situations control behavior and then to restructure the situation to promote the desired behaviors.**

For example, in a restaurant, a dessert cart often is brought to the table after dinner to allow customers to decide what to have for dessert. Some persons may not be able to "control themselves" and not order and eat a dessert. If overeating is a problem, the person who is aware of the stimulus control that the dessert cart exerts can avoid the temptation. After dinner, the person may decline the waiter's invitation to see the dessert cart and thereby control the response (eating dessert) he or she does not wish to perform. It may thus be easier to avoid the dessert by removing the stimuli that increase the likelihood of ordering it.

Similarly, a college student may have difficulty studying in his or her dormitory room. When he or she sits down to study, there may be a radio on the desk, letters from home, and a telephone. A chatting roommate may also make studying difficult. All of these events are associated with nonstudy behaviors (e.g., listening to the radio, reading letters or writing replies, chatting on the phone, listening to a roommate). To increase the likelihood of studying, the student might rely upon stimulus control. Specifically, the student might take just the materials necessary for studying and go to a cubicle in the university library where there are no distractions. Studying should be much more likely to occur because the library would not include the stimuli that compete with concentration.

Stimulus control is a self-control technique because the client can apply knowledge of the concept to alter behavior. Using stimulus control ordinarily requires that someone consult with the client to explain how stimulus control operates and to help the client identify events that control or fail to control his or her behavior. As the client understands and applies the basic concept, he or she can extend the range of behaviors that are altered. The client actually carries out the procedure to change the stimulus control.

The crucial elements to remember about using stimulus control are:
- Require the client to self-observe to obtain information about the occurrence of behaviors to be changed.
- The client needs to observe the situations in which behavior occurs or fails to occur. The frequency of behavior in particular situations (stimulus conditions) is critical.
- Identify the situations or circumstances in which the desired behavior is to occur.

If the appropriate behavior is to be developed in a situation, have the client begin to perform the response in that situation. Be sure there are no distracting stimuli that will lead to undesired responses in the situation. If inappropriate behavior is to be eliminated in a situation, have the client begin to perform the new response in that situation (see Alternate Response Training).

The use of stimulus control is described below.

*Nicki had been seeing Mr. Beck, the high school counselor, for about a month. Her grades had dropped off, and there had been some problems with alcohol. Her friends were basically pretty good but recently they had begun to hang out behind an old warehouse. There wasn't anything to do there and every time it would turn into a drinking party. Nicki really didn't want to drink, and she didn't like the effect of alcohol on her friends. But she found it very hard, in fact impossible, to say **no** when all the other kids started to drink.*

One suggestion her counselor made was to get the group to spend their time away from the warehouse. Mr. Beck helped Nicki come up with some other activities she could suggest to the group such as roller skating, bowling, listening to records at her house, so that they wouldn't end up at the warehouse drinking. As the weeks passed, Mr. Beck continued to support Nicki's attempts at controlling her environment. Her life gradually came back to normal.

Below please describe what stimulus control means when used as a self-control technique. _____

_____
_____
_____

You should have said that stimulus control means identifying situations and conditions that control one's behavior and then altering or restructuring the environment so desired behaviors are more likely to occur.

The situation described below shows how stimulus control is used to alter the behavior.

As Mr. and Mrs. Benson were cleaning up after dinner one night, a discussion started about how the family never seemed to talk any more or be together very much. They used to eat dinner in the dining room and have the best conversations. But recently they had been eating in front of the television to catch the news.

Pretend you are the Bensons and describe how you would use stimulus control to solve the problem. _____

_____
_____
_____

PROCEDURE VI—Self-Instruction Training

People often say things privately to themselves that may influence their behavior. For example, after making a mistake or doing something incorrectly, persons often reprimand themselves, swear, or even call themselves nasty names. After doing something well, positive statements are often made such as "I did it," "fantastic," and so on.

Not all of the things that persons say to themselves are consequences. Many of the statements are prompts or events that come before the behavior. Individuals often give themselves instructions or rehearse how they shoud perform. For example, before going into a job interview with a prospective employer, persons may privately remind themselves how to behave, what to say, and what to avoid. The statements serve as prompts to help initiate the desired behavior. Other statements may take the form of rehearsal as individuals practice what they may say and what employers might say.

Self-statements are most often private. Other persons cannot hear them or see that the person is stating them. We know of their occurrence because we ourselves make such statements, and because we often see other persons make such statements out loud. For example, when a tennis player makes a mistake and loses a crucial game, we often hear at a distance the obscene self-statement that the player makes.

We are generally familiar with the fact that instructions and statements (e.g., praise, approval) delivered by others control behavior. Most persons are less familiar with the fact that self-instructions and self-statements also can control behavior. Self-instruction training has been used as a self-control technique. **With self-instruction training, the client is trained to control his or her behavior by making suggestions and specific comments that guide behavior in a fashion similar to being instructed by someone else.**

For example, children who act impulsively often make mistakes in their academic work and perform tasks too quickly. Self-instruction training can be used to help those children perform tasks more carefully. When children are confronted with a task, they may be taught to ask themselves certain questions that will help them complete the task correctly. In class, the child may be trained to ask himself or herself certain questions (e.g., "What does the teacher want me to do?"). The child then learns to answer the question by specifying the task carefully (e.g., "I am supposed to copy words off the board exactly as they are written"). Then, during the task, the child can check to see how the task is being performed by asking and answering other questions (e.g., "How well am I doing so far? Is this the way it should be done?").

Self-instruction training is a self-control technique because clients can apply it freely to new situations they encounter. However, the procedure usually requires careful training in individual or group sessions so that one can learn what statements can be used to alter behavior. The statements vary for the behaviors that are to be changed and the age and abilities of the clients. For example, adults who have disturbing thoughts they cannot rid themselves of have been trained to say "stop" to themselves. This can be effective in eliminating those thoughts. Children who are afraid of the dark have been trained to make self-statements to help them cope with darkness. Also, psychiatric patients who occasionally speak irrationally have been trained to remind themselves to speak coherently by self-instructing themselves not to repeat themselves and to pay attention to what others say.

The crucial elements to remember about using self-instruction training are:
- Require the client to self-observe to obtain information about the occurrence of the behavior.
- Develop a short list of things the client can say to himself or herself to help initiate the desired behavior. The statements may include things to say to avoid undesirable behaviors (e.g., "Remember, I should not answer the questions before reading the little story"), to develop the correct behavior (e.g., "I need to read each answer carefully before deciding which one is right") and to check on how the task is going ("How am I doing so far?").
- Build a self-evaluation component into the self-statements. When the client does complete the behavior correctly, he or she should administer self-praise (e.g., "Gee, I did a good job!"). Alternatively, when mistakes are made, feedback should be included (e.g., "There are these things wrong with what I did. To do better next time, I should . . . ."). Thus, self-instruction training can incorporate the advantages of self-reinforcement and self-punishment to develop appropriate behavior.

The use of self-instruction to alter behavior is described below.

Mrs. Watson reached to turn off her alarm. "Oh, no." she groaned, "not another day with those students." It had gotten to the point where she disliked going to work. Her fourth grade students had become more and more disruptive and were spending less and less time attending to their schoolwork. She had tried keeping them in from recess, or after school but that had not helped. She had tried assigning extra work but that also did not help. She had noticed that when the students had been given more say in decisions they had done a better job. Maybe a self-instruction procedure would work.

She decided to teach her students to use self-instructions while performing different tasks and assignments. Each child was taught to make statements about what he or she was supposed to do; what were his or her possible assignments; what should be his or her choice; and how to evaluate themselves. The children were told to say these instructions to themselves, first aloud, then in a whisper and, finally, to themselves. By the end of a month of training, the children were completing more and more of their assignments.

To ensure understanding, describe self-instruction training as a self-control technique. _____

You are correct if you said that self-instruction training means teaching a person to control his or her own behavior by saying things (i.e., specific commands or statements) that guide behavior in a specific fashion.

The vignette below describes a situation where self-instructions could be applied. Please read it and work out a self-instruction training program.

Jeff was an excellent swimmer but his real desire was to be a high diver. He had done well in the springboard competition but was experiencing more and more difficulty as he tried the more complex dives from higher platforms. His problem seemed to come as he started out on the platform. He would become very frustrated and found it difficult to concentrate on the particular moves needed for the different dives from the higher platform. He was determined to overcome this problem.

Describe a self-instruction training program for Jeff. _____

Guidelines for Using Self-Control

Six different self-control procedures have been described. When implementing these six techniques either alone or in various combinations, it is important to be aware of the following points.

1. Be sure to continue to monitor the progress of the behavior you are trying to change. This is necessary to evaluate how well the self-control program is working and what changes, if any, should be made in the program.
2. Make sure that the self-control procedure the person is going to use is one he or she can carry out in terms of age, IQ, and level of functioning. In the beginning of the program, the client may be responsible for only a small part of the program. Perhaps the client might begin by only self-observing the target behaviors. But as the client becomes more successful, he or she can take more responsibility until he or she is self-administering all aspects of the procedure.
3. Self-control techniques are especially useful in situations where other persons (i.e., parents, teachers, staff) are unavailable to carry out other behavioral procedures.
4. Self-control procedures can be used effectively as part of a maintenance procedure following other programs. When a person leaves a program where external agents such as parents or teachers administered the consequences, self-control procedures may be used to maintain behavior change.
5. When teaching self-control procedures to clients be sure to stress the importance of using what they have learned in new situations with new and different problems.
6. When clients begin to use self-control techniques it is important that they be checked to see if they are adhering to the requirements and contingencies of the self-control program.
7. Be sure that whenever self-punishment is used that it is part of other self-control procedures that involve reinforcement for appropriate behavior.
8. To facilitate client adherence to a self-control regimen it is useful to enlist the help of other persons from the client's environment (i.e., parents, peers, etc.). These persons should praise the client when the client applies the procedures to himself or herself. This is especially important at the beginning of the self-control program.

Monitoring Behavior

To evaluate the effectiveness of the self-control procedures, it is necessary for the behaviors to be carefully monitored. This monitoring involves clearly defining the behavior the person wants to increase or decrease. Along with the definition, how often the behavior occurs must be measured. Different methods of observing and counting behaviors can be used.

One common procedure is to keep a simple tally or frequency count of the behavior when it occurs. Some behaviors easily counted this way include swearing, smoking or arguments. Sometimes it is more appropriate to determine the percent of time one performs a specified behavior. For example, the percent of time students complete assignments might be observed. In other cases, timing how long a behavior lasts may be more important. Getting ready in the morning, falling asleep at night, and length of lunch breaks are examples where timing the behavior may be useful.

Other manuals in this series discuss methods of measuring behavior. These methods can be readily used to monitor self-control programs where the client serves as the person who keeps track of his or her behaviors. (See **How to Use Systematic Attention and Approval** and **How to Use Planned Ignoring**, by R. Vance Hall and Marilyn C. Hall.)

Many persons find it helpful and informative to get a visual picture of the behavior being measured. This can be done by graphing the behavior. From the graph one can quickly determine if the self-control program has been effective in altering behavior. For example, a fourth-grade teacher wanted to increase the number of times one of her students raised his hand to talk in class. Each time the student raised his hand to speak, she recorded it. She continued recording for one week before she started her program. This week of recording is referred to as the baseline period and is needed to determine how often the behavior is occurring before a program is implemented. Following the baseline period, she started a self-control program that involved self-observations and self-reinforcement where the student recorded on a chart at his desk the number of times he raised his hand before talking and then posted a colored star or sticker beside each mark. The following graph shows his behavior during baseline and during self-observation with self-reinforcement.

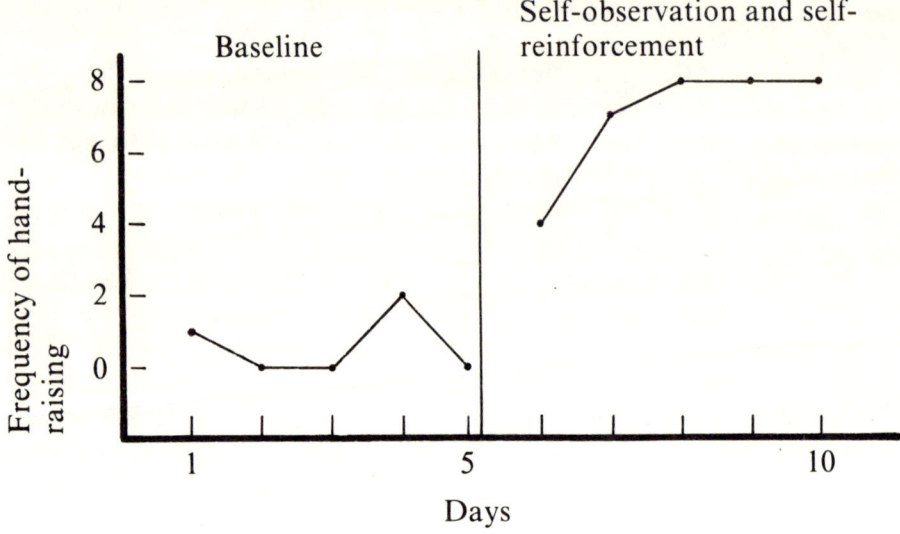

Handling Problems That Arise

Not all self-control programs will be immediately successful. In instances where problems arise, several things can be done. The first step is to determine whether the program is being carried out as designed. Is the person administering the correct consequences for the correct behaviors or performing the correct response in appropriate situations? Before changing a program, be certain that the program has been fairly tried.

If adherence to the program is the problem, then some system of prompts or praise for compliance should be implemented. These extra prompts or praise can then be faded as the person learns to self-administer and monitor himself or herself.

When self-reinforcement does not appear to be working, the problem may be that the positive consequences are not things the person truly desires or enjoys. Similiarly, self-punishment may not be working because the consequences are not sufficiently aversive. It may be possible to continue self-reinforcement or self-punishment if the positive or negative consequences are altered.

As mentioned at various points throughout this manual, combining two or more self-control procedures can be very effective in changing behavior. Self-reinforcement is especially easy to combine with other self-control techniques to help make them more effective.

In some cases where self-control does not appear to be working, the problem may be that the behavior being treated is one that initially needs to be treated by using other behavioral techniques such as time-out, systematic attention, and point programs. Once these are successful, then one might shift to self-control procedures to continue behavior change or to maintain the change.

Planning Your Own Self-Control Program

When learning a new skill, it is essential to practice the skill. To give you an opportunity to practice what you have learned about self-control procedures, plan and carry out a self-control program to either increase or decrease a behavior you want changed.

To begin, define the behavior you want to change. _____
_____
_____
_____
_____

Describe the **self-control procedure(s)** you chose to use. _____
_____
_____
_____

How did you monitor your self-control program? _____
_____
_____
_____

Describe how your program worked. _____
_____
_____
_____

What if any problems did you encounter? _____
_____
_____
_____

Were you able to overcome them? If so, how? _____
_____
_____
_____

Think about and list other behaviors or situations you would like to change and define which self-control procedures would be appropriate.

References

Ballard, K. D., and Glynn, T. Behavioral self-management in story writing with elementary school children. **Journal of Applied Behavior Analysis,** 1975, **8,** 387-398.

Beiman, I., Graham, L. E., and Ciminero, A. R. Self-control progressive relaxation training as an alternative nonpharmacological treatment for essential hypertension: Therapeutic effects in the natural environment. **Behaviour Research and Therapy,** 1978, **16,** 371-375.

Bellack, A. S. A comparison of self-reinforcement and self-monitoring in a weight reduction program. **Behavior Therapy,** 1976, **7,** 68-75.

Bornstein, P. H., and Quevillon, R. P. The effects of a self-instructional package on overactive preschool boys. **Journal of Applied Behavior Analysis,** 1976, **9,** 179-188.

Hall, R. V., and Hall, M. C. **How to use systematic attention and approval.** Lawrence, KS: H & H Enterprises, Inc., 1980.

Hall, R. V., and Hall, M. C. **How to use planned ignoring.** Lawrence, KS: H & H Enterprises, Inc., 1980.

Herbert, E. W., and Baer, D. M. Training parents as behavior modifiers: Self-recording of contingent attention. **Journal of Applied Behavior Analysis,** 1972, **5,** 139-149.

Kanfer, F. H., Karoly, P., and Newman, A. Reduction of children's fear of the dark by competence-related and situational threat-related verbal cues. **Journal of Consulting and Clinical Psychology,** 1975, **43,** 251-258.

Kazdin, A. E. **Behavior modification in applied settings** (second edition). Homewood, IL: Dorsey, 1980.

Lovitt, T. C. and Esveldt-Dawson, K. A. Academic response rate as a function of teacher and self-imposed contingencies. **Journal of Applied Behavior Analysis,** 1969, **2,** 49-53.

Mahoney, M. J., and Thoresen, C. E. (Eds.), **Self-control: Power to the person.** Monterey, California: Brooks/Cole, 1974.

Meichenbaum, D. H., and Goodman, J. Training impulsive children to talk to themselves: A means of developing self-control. **Journal of Abnormal Psychology,** 1971, **77,** 115-126.

Stuart, R. B. (Ed.), **Behavioral self-management: Strategies, techniques, and outcomes.** New York: Brunner/Mazel, 1977.

Wilson, G. T., Leaf, R. C., and Nathan, P. E. The aversive control of excessive alcohol consumption by chronic alcoholics in the laboratory setting. **Journal of Applied Behavior Analysis,** 1975, **8,** 13-26.